Adult Coloring Book
Designs by Iva Oceanbringer

Relaxation and Stress Relief through Animals, Mandalas, Flowers, Doodles, Patterns, Shapes

IVA OCEANBRINGER

ISBN-10: 1979654557
ISBN-13: 978-1979654555

DEDICATION

This book is dedicated to my family, especially my 15-month-old son and my lovely husband. All the hard work and sleepless nights pay off when I see your smiles. I love you both from the bottom of my heart!

THANK YOUR FOR PURCHASING THIS BOOK

This is my very first Adult Coloring Book. I would love to stay in touch with you. You can visit my official website **www.iva-oceanbringer.com** and subscribe to my newsletter, to receive special offers, coupons and get the latest news about my new coloring books.

Happy coloring!

Many lovely greetings

Iva Oceanbringer

P. S. Follow me on my social media channels:

facebook.com/Iva.Oceanbringer

twitter.com/ivaoceanbringer

instagram.com/iva.oceanbringer

Tip: I would recommend coloring pencils. If you like to use felt pens or something else, make sure to put some sheets of paper in between.

THIS BOOK BELONGS TO

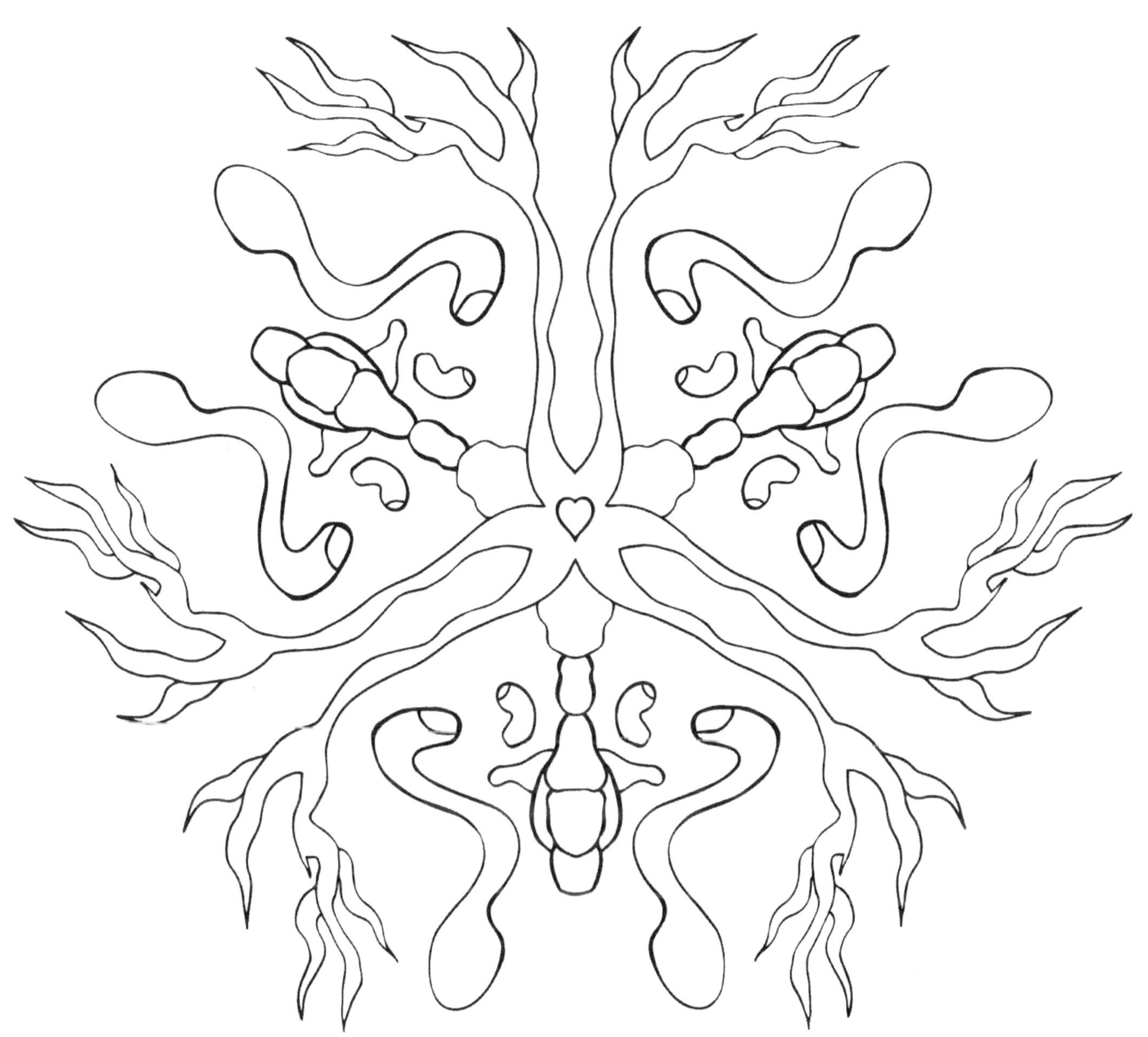

MY NOTES

Relax your mind and use this space for your personal notes.

ABOUT THE AUTHOR

Iva Oceanbringer is a mom and a wife and she works in the field of Health Care Management. In her free time she loves to illustrate coloring books for adults and children. Iva Oceanbringer is convinced that coloring books have a healing power because they help you to relax and free your mind from stress.

If you'd like to learn more about Iva, you can visit her website and subscribe to her newsletter to receive special offers, coupons, and latest news about her new coloring books.

www.iva-oceanbringer.com

facebook.com/Iva.Oceanbringer

twitter.com/ivaoceanbringer

instagram.com/iva.oceanbringer

www.ingramcontent.com/pod-product-compliance
Lightning Source LLC
Chambersburg PA
CBHW080850260726
48660CB00009B/3268